W9-AXM-374

STANDARD
OF LIVING

Andrew J. Milson, Ph.D.
Content Consultant
University of Texas at Arlington

Acknowledgments

Grateful acknowledgment is given to the authors, artists, photographers, museums, publishers, and agents for permission to reprint copyrighted material. Every effort has been made to secure the appropriate permission. If any omissions have been made or if corrections are required, please contact the Publisher.

Instructional Consultant: Christopher Johnson, Evanston, Illinois

Teacher Reviewer: Patricia Lewis, Humble Middle School, Humble, Texas

Photographic Credits

Cover, Inside Front Cover, Title Page ©Yu Chu Di/Redlink/Redlink/Corbis. **3** (bg) ©Stockbyte/Getty Images. **4** (bg) ©Paul Hardy/Corbis. **6** (bg) ©Ludovic Maisant/Hemis/Corbis. **8** (bg) Mapping Specialists. **10** (bg) ©Carlos Cazalis/Carlos Cazalis/Corbis. **13** (bg) ©Julie Dermansky/Corbis. **14** (bg) ©Technical Sgt. James L. Harper Jr./US Air Force/Handout/Digital Still Asset/Corbis. (tl) ©ZUMA Wire Service/Alamy. **16** (bg) ©Jeremy Horner/Corbis. **18** (t) ©Yadid Levy/Robert Harding World Imagery/Corbis. **20** (bg) ©Ali Kabas/Picade LLC/Alamy. **22** (bg) ©Aaron Kisner courtesy of Vital Voices Global Partnership/PR NEWSWIRE/Newscom. (cl) ©Philip Andrews/National Geographic Society. **25** (bg) ©Philip Andrews/National Geographic Society. **27** (t) ©Jim West/Alamy. **28** (tr) ©Photos and Co/Lifesize/Getty Images. **30** (tr) ©Philip Andrews/National Geographic Society. (br) ©Carlos Cazalis/Carlos Cazalis/Corbis. **31** (bl) ©LeoFFreitas/Flickr/Getty Images. (bg) ©Stockbyte/Getty Images. (br) ©Paul Hardy/Corbis. (tr) ©Ludovic Maisant/Hemis/Corbis.

For permission to use material from this text or product, submit all requests online at www.cengage.com/permissions.

Further permissions questions can be emailed to permissionrequest@cengage.com.

Visit National Geographic Learning online at www.NGSP.com.

Visit our corporate website at www.cengage.com.

Printed in the USA.

RR Donnelley, Jefferson City, MO

ISBN: 978-07362-97660

12 13 14 15 16 17 18 19 20 21

10 9 8 7 6 5 4 3 2 1

HOW WE LIVE

People who live in the world's most populated areas, such as New York City, New York, in the United States, have access to a vast, complex network of goods and services, but only if they can afford them.

HOW DOES STANDARD OF LIVING AFFECT PEOPLE'S LIVES?

One family in a suburb lives in a big house. The children attend school and plan to go to college. They eat good food and get regular medical checkups. Another family in a rural area lives in a small hut. Often, the children go to bed hungry. No one in the family has ever attended school or visited a doctor or dentist.

These families live worlds apart in **standard of living**— the level of available income, goods, and services in a place. Different levels within and between countries separate people and affect where and how they live.

People living below the poverty line would not be able to afford even simple luxuries, such as buying flowers at a popular London street market.

WHAT IS STANDARD OF LIVING?

To measure standard of living, economists look at whether people can afford the basics: clean water, food, shelter, and clothing. Depending on where they live, some people can barely meet their needs while others enjoy luxuries.

Affording the basics depends largely on **income**, which is the amount of money a person makes in a certain period of time. A low-wage earner in one place might be considered a high-wage earner in another. This is because the cost of living varies from place to place. **Cost of living** is the amount of money required to maintain a certain standard of living.

Other factors that determine standard of living include access to education and health care. Level of education influences a person's income. Access to health care affects **life expectancy**, which is the number of years that a person in a particular group or place can expect to live. People with higher standards of living generally live longer lives.

COMPARING STANDARDS OF LIVING

One way to compare standards of living among countries is to look at the number of people living below the poverty line. The **poverty line** is the minimum income required to meet basic needs. In 2010, the poverty line for a family of four in the United States was $22,314. About 15 percent lived below the poverty line in 2010, compared to 65 percent in Honduras, and less than 2 percent in Taiwan.

What do these kinds of statistics say about people's lives? The simplest answer is that most people can meet their basic needs in wealthier countries. On the following pages, you'll read about two countries—Haiti and Turkey—with different standards of living. You'll learn about how this difference affects people's lives.

COUNTRIES WITH THE HIGHEST STANDARD OF LIVING

1 NORWAY
2 AUSTRALIA
3 NETHERLANDS
4 UNITED STATES
5 NEW ZEALAND
6 CANADA
7 IRELAND
8 LIECHTENSTEIN
9 GERMANY
10 SWEDEN

Source: United Nations HDI 2011 Rankings

Explore the Issue

1. **Summarize** How is standard of living measured?

2. **Analyze Effects** How does standard of living affect people's lives?

Value of all goods produced in a year, divided by a country's population (U.S. Dollars, 2010)

- more than 40,000
- 20,000–39,999
- 10,000–19,999
- 5,000–9,999
- less than 5,000
- no data

NORTH ATLANTIC OCEAN

NORTH AMERICA

NORTH ATLANTIC OCEAN

ALBANIA Many people live in rural poverty, making Albania one of Europe's poorest countries.

UNITED STATES Natural resources, a stable political system, and an educated workforce have helped most U.S. citizens achieve a high standard of living.

CASE STUDY 1

HAITI Political instability and natural disasters have made Haiti the poorest country in the Americas.

SOUTH AMERICA

SOUTH PACIFIC OCEAN

SOUTH ATLANTIC OCEAN

Explore the Issue

1. **Interpret Maps** What are two continents with countries that produce less than $5,000 per year per person?

2. **Analyze Effects** How does education affect standard of living?

und the World

ARCTIC OCEAN

EUROPE

NORTH PACIFIC OCEAN

ASIA

AFRICA

BANGLADESH The country is overpopulated. Thirty-two percent of the people live below the poverty line.

CASE STUDY 2

TURKEY Economic reforms and more private industry have helped to raise the country's standard of living.

INDIAN OCEAN

AUSTRALIA

BURKINA FASO Less than one-quarter of the population can read and almost half the people live below the poverty line.

N
W   E
S

0	1,000	2,000 Miles
0	1,000	2,000 Kilometers

ANTARCTICA

HAITI'S STRUGGLE
to Overcome Poverty

The lives of Haitians were made more difficult after the devastating earthquake in 2010. Left homeless, many families made camp near Haiti's airport.

BARELY GETTING BY

Before the destructive earthquake of 2010, many people in Haiti, an island of Hispaniola (hihs-puhn-YOH-luh) in the Caribbean Sea, lived in poverty. Haiti is the poorest country in the Americas. It has limited resources, and its economy depends too much on agriculture. Today over 72 percent of the population lives on less than $2.00 per day. Over 58 percent of income is spent on food.

Haiti's poor soil cannot support many crops. Pierre Alexis Cantave (pee-AIR uh-LEK-sis kan-TAHV) is a farmer in the Central Plateau region of Haiti. Although he owns a large tract of land, most of it is unusable for growing crops. He cannot afford to improve the soil. The worn-out fields do not produce enough crops to feed his wife and five children. Cantave's situation is not unusual. Nearly two-thirds of all Haitians are **subsistence farmers**. They plant crops and keep livestock to feed their own families. In recent years, they have not been able to produce enough food for themselves.

Their struggle has not gone unnoticed. Feed the Future, a program of the United States Agency for International Development (USAID), teaches farmers to plant crops, such as mango and cocoa trees, that can grow in poor soils and help restore eroded hillsides. The program also works with the government to help small farms and businesses to grow.

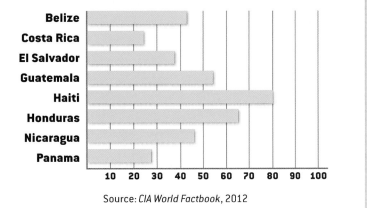

PERCENTAGE OF POPULATION LIVING BELOW POVERTY LINE IN CENTRAL AMERICA

Source: *CIA World Factbook*, 2012

PROBLEMS IN THE PAST AND PRESENT

Haiti's past problems have helped to create lasting, deep poverty. In the 1600s and 1700s, French planters ruled Haiti. The planters damaged the land through **deforestation**—the process of cutting and clearing trees for fuel or farmland. Large plantations of sugarcane soon wore out the soil.

In the late 1700s, the slaves began a revolution against the French. In 1804, Haiti gained independence but not prosperity. Frequent changes in government, poor rulers, and political violence have kept the people poor and suffering.

Today, high crime rates and a lack of education slow progress in Haiti. For example, only 53 percent of Haitians are **literate**. This means that just over half the population can read and write. Another problem is the country's **infant mortality rate**. This is the number of infant deaths for every 1,000 live births. In Haiti, the infant mortality rate is very high at 52 deaths for every 1,000 births.

In addition to the high crime rates, poor soil, low education levels, and lack of adequate health care, half of all Haitians do not have access to clean water, a critical, basic need. As a result, the risk of catching diseases through contamination of water and food sources is very high. Life expectancy for adults in Haiti is only 63 years.

DAMAGED BY DISASTER

To make matters even worse, Haiti has experienced many natural disasters. For example, on January 12, 2010, a massive earthquake struck Haiti. Several strong aftershocks soon followed. Many government offices, hospitals, schools, and power plants collapsed. Hundreds of thousands of people were **displaced**, or forced out of their homes to live in tents and temporary shelters. The government estimates that more than 230,000 people died in the earthquakes. Survivors had difficulty getting help.

After the earthquake, people around the world responded. Many donated money to relief agencies, such as the International Red Cross. Others responded by traveling to Haiti to help the survivors. Countries large and small sent medical supplies and doctors.

Time Line of Disasters in Haiti

August 5, 1980
Hurricane Allen kills 220 Haitians.

September 9, 1997
A ferry sinks, killing 300 to 400 people.

August and September, 2008
Three major tropical storms kill 423 Haitians. More than 850,000 people lose homes or businesses.

1980 1990 2000 2010

February 18, 1993
A ferry sinks, killing an estimated 700 people.

September 23, 2004
Tropical storm Jeanne kills more than 3,000 people.

January 12, 2010
A powerful earthquake kills an estimated 230,000 people and leaves one million more homeless.

Source: Fort Lauderdale *Sun Sentinel*, 2010 and U.S. Department of State

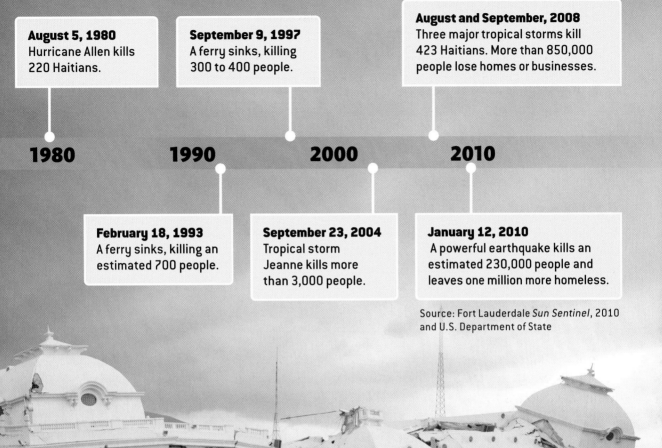

Survivors of the 2010 earthquake seek help outside the badly damaged presidential palace in Port-au-Prince, the capital city of Haiti.

Haitian girls jump rope near the education and feeding center in Port-au-Prince, Haiti. Rebuilding schools can help improve Haiti's standard of living.

After the 2010 earthquake, American aircraft drop urgently needed supplies by parachute into Port-au-Prince and surrounding areas.

HELPING HAITI REBUILD

In 2011, Haitians elected a new president. At the request of President Michel Martelly, international aid organizations have sent financial aid, construction equipment, medical supplies, experts, and volunteers to help Haitians rebuild.

Recovering from such a terrible disaster is a long process. In addition to relief and recovery projects, some organizations help the country in reaching its long-term goals. One such organization is the Clinton Bush Haiti Fund, organized by two former U.S. presidents. To help Haiti improve its economy, the fund promotes goals like these:

- Help artisans sell their goods internationally.
- Make loans available to new business owners.
- Bring modern communication technologies, such as the Internet, to rural areas.

INVESTING IN EDUCATION

Another important way to raise Haiti's standard of living is to improve education. Countries need educated workers to develop the industries and technology that bring progress. Unfortunately, the 2010 earthquake destroyed half the schools in Haiti.

The United Nations Educational, Scientific and Cultural Organization (UNESCO) sponsors projects to rebuild schools and train teachers. An educated workforce is needed to rebuild the land, the communities, and the economy.

Pierre Alexis Cantave believes in education. He attended a workshop that was sponsored by the U.S. Agency for International Development (USAID). There he learned how to grow better crops. "My participation in USAID's program has changed my life," he says. Because of his experience, Cantave believes education can transform his village and his country.

Explore the Issue

1. **Find Main Ideas** What problems helped to create Haiti's poverty?

2. **Draw Conclusions** What recent developments might help to improve Haiti's standard of living?

Turkey's SOLID MIDDLE CLA

It has become easier for people in Turkey to own their own businesses, such as this carpet shop in Istanbul. Privately owned businesses help to improve Turkey's standard of living.

BUILDING A BUSINESS

Saffet Arslan (SAH-fit AHR-sluhr) of Turkey is a modern-day success story. He was born the son of a carpet maker, a traditional Turkish occupation. When Arslan finished elementary school, his family needed him to find a job. By the age of 14, he was working as a cabinet maker in a shop. Many people would have stayed in that position their whole lives, but Arslan wanted more. He started his own cabinet shop and eventually opened several branches.

Arslan didn't stop there. In 1991, he started his own furniture company. By making folding beds—a product in high demand—business took off. Arslan succeeded for three reasons. He worked hard, he made smart business decisions, and he lives in Turkey, a country that is experiencing rapid economic growth.

BUILDING A MODERN COUNTRY

For 600 years, Turkey was the center of the Ottoman Empire, a powerful state that ruled much of southwest Asia, North Africa, and southeastern Europe. Over time, the empire grew weak, and it finally broke apart after World War I.

A revolution broke out in 1923, and Mustafa Kemal (moo-stah-FAH keh-MAHL), later called Atatürk (AT-uh-turk), founded modern Turkey. Atatürk's government instituted many progressive reforms that improved the people's standard of living. These included a modern law code, more equality for women, and education opportunities. The government also provided funds to develop industry.

However, when the government funded industries, it also took greater control of them. For example, it established many rules and regulations, which hurt Turkey's economy. By the 1970s, Turkey experienced problems. These included high unemployment and **inflation**—a period of rising prices for goods and services. The country bought more goods from other countries than it traded. Changes were needed to keep Turkey on the road to progress.

Over the next 20 years, Turkey's leaders changed old laws so more people such as Arslan could start businesses. As a result, Turkey's economy grew. The country also reduced taxes on goods coming into the country. Doing so opened more trade with other countries.

REFORMS LEAD TO GROWTH

Beginning in the 1980s, Turkey began to make important economic changes. The government stopped regulating businesses so much, and more businesses became privately owned. Privately owned businesses like Arslan's are usually more successful because they can respond more quickly to their customers' needs.

Another reform that helped business was reducing the level of **bureaucracy**. Bureaucracy is a system of government that has many officials, rules, and forms. The government also eased trade restrictions and reduced taxes on goods.

These reforms made it much easier for people such as Saffet Arslan to start their own companies. New businesses meant new income opportunities for the owners and more jobs in the community. As a result, Turkey has developed a solid middle class. The middle class helped Turkey's economy to grow in more areas.

Vendors and shoppers fill Eminonu Square, a marketplace in Istanbul, Turkey. In a stable economy, more people are able to produce, sell, and buy goods.

TACKLING THE INFLATION MONSTER

In spite of these changes, inflation remained a problem in Turkey. In fact, during 1997, prices nearly doubled in a single year! That meant money bought only half as much as it had in the previous year. Such steep inflation destroys the value of money and makes it hard for people and businesses to buy what they need. Something had to be done.

The International Monetary Fund (IMF) is an organization of 187 countries that promotes financial stability and economic growth. It worked with Turkey to control runaway inflation. Following IMF recommendations, the government made changes to its spending and taxation. It also continued to make economic reforms.

After an 18-month economic program, prices stabilized. In 2009, inflation dropped to the lowest it had been in 34 years. Rising prices of goods and services slowed down and leveled off. Once again, the economy was able to grow.

VALUE OF GOODS AND SERVICES PRODUCED IN TURKEY, PER PERSON	
YEAR	PER CAPITA
2002	$3,553
2004	$5,833
2006	$7,687
2008	$10,298
2010	$10,094

Source: World Bank

"Turkey is neither east or west.
We are moving in our own direction."
—Tugce Erbad, a student of international finance in Turkey

Turkish goods bound for foreign ports are loaded on barges in the Port of Istanbul. Trade with other countries has helped Turkey's economy.

FINDING NEW ENERGY

Turkey also wants to decrease its dependence on oil. While the country has significant coal deposits, it has hardly any oil. As a result, Turkey imports oil for much of its energy needs. This situation can cause problems as oil prices tend to change frequently. A rise in oil prices makes it more expensive to produce and ship goods. Rising costs also reduce the profits that business can earn.

In May 2006, a newly built oil pipeline that ran from the Caspian Sea in Azerbaijan (ahz-ur-by-JAHN) across Turkey opened. The oil flows to a Turkish port on the Mediterranean, where it is shipped to Europe. Additional pipelines will move natural gas from Central Asia across Turkey. These projects are helping to meet Turkey's energy needs today. To reduce the country's need for oil, the government also encourages industries to switch to **renewable energy** sources, such as solar and wind power. These natural power sources do not harm the environment.

JOINING THE EUROPEAN UNION (EU)

Because Turkey lies between Europe and Asia, it wants to strengthen its ties to other countries. In 1999, the European Union (EU) accepted Turkey as a member candidate. However, in order to become a full member, Turkey will have to change its laws, regulations, and policies to match EU standards. This is a lengthy and difficult process.

If Turkey does join the EU, it will have free trade with EU members and the choice of sharing a common currency. However, since requesting membership, an unstable economy in Europe has delayed progress. In addition, public opinion among Turks has changed. By 2010, fewer than 40 percent of Turkey's citizens wanted to join the EU. Unless public interest grows, joining the EU may not happen. For now, Turkey remains independent and confident in shaping a bright future.

Explore the Issue

1. **Find Main Ideas** How did steep inflation hurt Turkey's economy?

2. **Find Details** In what ways do privately owned businesses help Turkey's economy?

Providing Education Opportunities

Maasai children eagerly gather around teacher
Kakenya Ntaiya to hear a humorous story.

EDUCATION FOR ALL

The Maasai (mah-SY) of East Africa have lived as nomads raising herds of cattle for hundreds of years, but the land can no longer adequately support their population. To help raise the Maasai's standard of living, which is low, the government of Kenya has encouraged them to settle in villages and on farms. Yet that step alone is not enough to lift them out of poverty.

Although Kenya requires all children to attend school for at least eight years, many Maasai families take their daughters out of school at age 13 so they can marry. Traditionally, the Maasai have not encouraged girls or women to continue their education. A determined young Maasai girl, Kakenya Ntaiya (kah-KEN-yuh nuh-tuh-EE-yuh), challenged this practice. Ntaiya, who today is a National Geographic Emerging Explorer, has taken extraordinary steps to improve education for girls in Kenya.

In developing countries, educating women tends to raise the people's standard of living. Educated women often have fewer children, which reduces overpopulation. **Overpopulation** is the condition of having more people than an area can support. It is one of the numerous reasons for low standards of living of the developing countries around the world.

A YOUNG GIRL'S DREAM

Born in a small Kenyan village, Ntaiya was the first of eight children. Her father worked in a distant city, and her mother labored in sugarcane fields. As the oldest child in the family, Ntaiya had to help with all the chores, work in the fields, and care for her siblings.

When she turned five, her parents announced her engagement to a village boy. This was the custom among traditional people of Kenya. But Ntaiya dreamed of becoming a teacher. So, she negotiated with her parents to be allowed to attend high school. In exchange for their permission, she told her parents that she would follow Maasai customs and study hard to earn good grades. True to her promise, Ntaiya achieved high grades and won a college scholarship to study in the United States. She looked forward to this exciting opportunity.

KEEPING A PROMISE

As Ntaiya prepared for college, her father became ill and could not work. Her family had no money to send Ntaiya overseas. Again she negotiated, this time with a village leader. She promised to use her education to help her people. The village worked hard to raise the money to send her to college, and Ntaiya kept her promise.

Ntaiya attended graduate school to earn an advanced degree in education. She also worked to achieve an ambitious plan—to build a girls' school in her village. In 2009, she opened the Academy for Girls, the first primary school for girls in that part of Kenya.

"I'm helping girls who cannot speak for themselves," Ntaiya explains. "Why should they go through the hardships I endured? They'll be stepping on my shoulders to move up the ladder—they're not going to start on the bottom."

In its first two years, the Academy enrolled 60 students. Ntaiya's goal is 150 students in grades four through eight. "We keep class sizes very small, so each girl receives a great deal of individual attention," Ntaiya says.

MAKING A DIFFERENCE

Kakenya Ntaiya raises money for her school by accepting invitations to speak with helping organizations all over the world. On her trips abroad, she shares the story of one girl's promise to her people. Because Ntaiya believes that education will empower the girls and their families, she is helping the Maasai shape a brighter future for themselves.

Kakenya Ntaiya succeeds because she set goals and works hard to achieve them. You, too, can set worthwhile goals and use your skills to make a difference in your world. The activity on the next two pages gives you a way to start.

Explore the Issue

1. **Draw Conclusions** Why is it important to educate Maasai girls beyond elementary school?

2. **Make Predictions** How might the work of Kakenya Ntaiya affect the standard of living of her people?

Kakenya Ntaiya shares a new book with Maasai children who are learning to read.

Organize a Food Drive

—and report your results

People in need are everywhere, not just in poor countries. Most communities have one or more food banks, places that collect and distribute food to people in need. Organize a food drive in your school, and donate the food to a community food bank. You'll be sharing food with people who really need it.

RESEARCH

- Find out the name, location, and phone number of a food bank in your community.

- Call the food bank to find out what kinds of food items they collect and to ask about their hours of operation.

- Make a list of the food you plan to collect. Be sure to include locally-grown produce and products.

ORGANIZE

- Prepare a flyer announcing your food drive. Indicate the date that you want students to bring their donations to school.

- Make copies of the flyers, and distribute them to students and teachers at your school.

- Obtain large boxes, label them, and place them in each classroom before the day of the food drive.

Community volunteers make a difference by serving meals to those in need.

DELIVER

- Collect the boxes of donated food.

- Ask volunteers to help inventory and organize the food into sturdy bags and boxes.

- Call the food bank and arrange the best time to deliver the food.

- Line up volunteers and adults at school to help load and transport the donated food to the food bank.

SHARE

- Announce the results of your food drive on your school's intercom, telling how many boxes of food you collected.

- Write a letter to your community newspaper, describing your efforts and encouraging others to donate to the food bank.

- Interview the director of the food bank to ask about the number of people the food bank serves. Share the information by giving talks to other classes at your school.

Research & WRITE

Argument

Write an Argumentative Article

What action would you like to see people take to improve the standard of living in the United States? Promote bicycling to improve our health? Increase the number of teacher aides to give individual attention to students who need help? Your task is to identify a way to improve our standard of living and to write a convincing argument promoting your claim.

RESEARCH

Use the Internet, books, and articles to find the following information:
- Data on the standard of living in the United States
- Suggested actions to improve the standard of living
- Evidence to support these suggestions

As you do your research, be sure to take good notes and keep track of your sources.

DRAFT

Review your notes and identify a course of action that you will recommend to others. It may be one you've researched, or it may be your own idea. Then write your draft.

- The first paragraph, or introduction, should get the reader's attention. Introduce your course of action, which is also known as your claim. State the reasons you support it.
- The second paragraph, or body, should provide clear reasons and relevant evidence supporting your claim that this course of action will help raise the standard of living. Use accurate, credible sources for your evidence.
- The third paragraph, or conclusion, should provide a statement that follows from and supports the argument you presented.

REVISE & EDIT

Read the draft carefully. Be sure your claim is supported with clear reasons and relevant evidence.

- Does the introduction get the attention of your audience and introduce your topic clearly?
- Does the body use words, phrases, and clauses that clarify the relationships among the claim, reasons, and evidence?
- Does your concluding statement follow from and support your argument?

Revise your draft to make your ideas clear. Check your writing for errors in grammar, spelling, and punctuation. Save your work.

PUBLISH & PRESENT

Now you are ready to publish and present your article. Add any images or graphs that enhance your ideas, and prepare a source list.

Then, print out your article, or write a clean copy by hand. Post it in the classroom or to your class website.

Visual GLOSSARY

literate

displaced

bureaucracy *n.*, a government system with many officials, rules, and forms

cost of living *n.*, the amount of money required to maintain a certain standard of living

deforestation *n.*, the process of cutting and clearing trees for fuel or farmland

displaced *v.*, forced out

income *n.*, the amount of money a person makes in a certain period time

infant mortality rate *n.*, the number of infant deaths per 1,000 live births

inflation *n.*, a period of rising prices for goods and services

life expectancy *n.*, the number of years that a person in a particular group or place can expect to live

literate *adj.*, able to read and write

overpopulation *n.*, a condition of having more people than an area can support

poverty line *n.*, the minimum income required to meet basic needs

renewable energy *n.*, a natural power source, such as the sun or wind

standard of living *n.*, the level of available income, goods, and services

subsistence farmer *n.*, one who plants crops or keeps livestock to feed one's own family

cost of living

standard of living

deforestation

INDEX

SKILLS